Grigore Arbore

B

ABBEY LIBRARY
LONDON

ellini

Translated from Romanian as published by
MERIDIANE PUBLISHING HOUSE
Bucharest, 1978
under the original title of
BELLINI
by
GRIGORE ARBORE

Translated into English by
ANDREEA GHEORGHIŢOIU

For anyone wishing to understand the extremely subtle evolution that led to the appearance in Venice of a school of painting with an original character in the context of the Italian Renaissance art as well as in the European one; for anyone wishing to understand how it was possible for a brilliant pleiad of first-rate artists such as Carpaccio, Giorgione, Titian or Veronese in the proud Venice to assert themselves and leave their indelible mark upon the figurative culture of the centuries to come, it is absolutely necessary and even imperative to refer to Giovanni Bellini's creation. For didactic reasons, the linear values characteristic of the art of the Tuscan masters are usually contrasted with the pictorial ones promoted by the Venetian school, gradually sublimated, in Titian's mature work more especially, where they express a gentle poetry and become a hymn to the warm, enveloping colour in which human beings, gods and nature itself can rest. The contrast is no doubt justified and whoever opens one of the numerous art treatises of the Cinquecento is bound to notice how frequently it is used.

The crystallization of the specific traits of the Venetian school of painting — which reached its acme in the 16th. century — is the outcome of a long period of development in which the historical epoch dominated by the personality of Giovanni Bellini played a very important role. His art could not be fully understood outside the general background against which Venetian art developed, a background whose specific features were determined by the peculiar political and geographic position of the city of the lagoon.

Situated at the crossways of important commercial routes, Venice was the main gate through which the cultural influences coming from the Eastern Empire penetrated into the West. Byzantine art, under its Venetian form gradually went through a process of reformation. We are thinking of the mosaics in the apse of the cathedral in Torcello, executed, the same as those on the lower part of the central apse of San Marco, towards the beginning of the 12th. century, as well as those in San Donato in Murano dating from the beginning of the 13th. century. We bring in support of this assertion the *Pala feriale* in St. Mark (about 1343) for instance, where the taste for the narrative is quite obvious, or the background of the altarpiece by Paolo Veneziano whose vivid chromatics already shows influences other than the traditional Byzantine ones upon Venetian painting. The Romanesque art coming from the *terraferma*, i.e. from the Italian peninsula, also influenced the city of the lagoon enriching the artistic Byzantine language. Frontal attitudes and brilliant immobility were to be replaced little by little by the integration of the figure into a spatial horizon. However, it is to be noted that between the 14th. and 15th. centuries, when the figurative culture of the Late Gothic massively penetrated into the city of the doges, painters like Lorenzo Veneziano (Paolo's pupil), Niccolò di Piero and later on Jacobello del Fiore, far from ignoring the ornamental function of colour, lent it new valences. Those were the years when the gorgeous Palazzo Ducale was built, years of fruitful contacts with the artistic milieu in Padua where, in the works of Giusto de'Menabuoi, Guariento, Altichiero, the influence of Giotto and other influences coming from Tuscany and

Emilia were grafted on the Venetian-Byzantine figurative culture, thus developing a peculiar sense of space. It is a fact that the Paduan masters contributed to the revival of the artistic climate of the epoch. On the other hand, during the first two decades of the 15th. century painters Gentile da Fabriano first (1408) and Pisanello later on (1415—1422), both outstanding representatives of the International Gothic, were in the service of the "Serenissima". Their presence left its mark on the work of the Gothic painter Jacobello del Fiore (died 1439), author of the *Coronation of the Virgin* at the Gallerie dell'Accademia; when in front of it one cannot help recalling on the spot the incomparable *Madonna della Misericordia* (at the Sansepolcro Picture Gallery) which Piero della Francesca painted a little later. The forms of the late Gothic still lasted in Venice through Giovanni d'Allemagna (died 1450) and his brother-in-law Antonio Vivarini (c. 1420 — c. 1484). In their works one can feel the presence of an incipient new stylistic, marking the transition from the Gothic forms to those of the early Renaissance. A distinguished critic, Roberto Longhi, maintained that Antonio Vivarini held the same place in Venetian art as Masolino did in the Florentine one. After Jacopo Bellini travelled to Florence in 1423, a new horizon opened up in Venetian painting, which was to be enriched in the following years by the very presence in Venice and Padua of the Tuscan masters Paolo Ucello and Filippo Lippi. However, a radical turning point was reached only with Giovanni Bellini in whose painting both the Byzantine and the Gothic features of Venetian art were to combine. It was only with him that the Byzantine chromatic harmonies, the ornamental quality of forms, the noble attitudes were to be structured in such a way as to form a spatial organization which will not exclude naturalistic elements and also grants special importance to the diffusion of light. With Giovanni Bellini, Venetian painting resolutely abandons strict plastic conventions, which does not mean, however, that we also witness a definitive break with the figurative tradition and conventions accepted so far. In the latter half of the 15th. century, painters such as Bartolomeo Vivarini (1432 — after 1491) or Carlo Crivelli (1430/1435 — c. 1500) carried on their activity in Venice; for them the stylistics of the Gothic were still a live memory, though with the former they were grafted on the expressive language of Castagno or with the latter, on the expressivity of Mantegna's figures as well as on the rational spirit of the compositions belonging to the Paduan school. Yet, at the end of the century, the means of expression peculiar to Giovanni's work had become the main guidemark in the orientation of Venetian painters. Truth to tell, the lyricism of Giovanni Bellini's work — whose warm colouring can be traced in some of the paintings of Alvise Vivarini (1445 — c. 1505) who was indebted both to the teachings of his uncle Bartolomeo and to the works Mantegna executed in Padua, and later on to Antonello da Messina — is in contrast all this time with the taste for the narrative and the gorgeous of his brother Gentile, the official illustrator of the developments in the history of Venice and head of a workshop painters visited quite often. Under Gentile's brush — it is sufficient in this respect to look at the scenes in *The Legend of the Cross* (Venice, Gallerie dell'Accademia), painted in the ninth decade for the Scuola di San Giovanni Evangelista — the city of the doges became a vast imaginary theatre in which the Aulic rituals took place, in which the background, the sky and architecture become as brilliant as precious stones. Carpaccio was to oscillate between the poesy of a sanctified reality on the one hand, and a fabulous world achieved by means of the plastic narrative on the other, synthetizing the artistic experience of both brothers. It is from Carpaccio's means of expression, from the paintings executed for the Scuola degli Schiavoni that we must start whenever we try to assess the significance of the landscape and of colour with Giorgione. But we must never forget that behind the experience of both, there looms the figure of the old Giambellino: he closes a chapter of Venetian art and opens another one: the artistic naturalism of the 16th. century.

That is why we consider quite natural to hold that the evolution of Venetian painting in the latter half of the 15th. century is tellingly synthesized in the work of Giovanni Bellini which can be compared with a receptacle collecting some of the most complex and fruitful experiences of a brilliant artistic tradition and the art of the time as well. Once assimilated and remoulded by the artist's sensitiveness, those experiences formed the basis of original poetics, permanently enriched not only by stimulating contacts but also by his aspiration to self-improvement, combined with an ever deeper understanding of the significances of the visible world and of their relationships with the work of art.

Giovanni Bellini belongs to the distinguished and generous family of artists who preserve unchanged their sensitiveness and creative power, while the hand and senses grow tired and through a natural process the eye finds it more and more difficult to filter light and distinguish colours. Yet before attaining the free and easy manner peculiar to the great masters freed from the burden of details and technical solutions through an exercise that had reached perfection, Giambellino's painting was to travel a road which may seem intricate in many respects, if we fail to take into account the fact that the originality of a plastic vision is not conditioned so much by the attraction some artistic creation exerts upon another, but by the artist's power to instill life into the suggestions coming from the outside, by viewing them from a different perspective, adopting them organically so as to lend them a specific dimension.

The initial seduction exerted by his father's art upon young Giovanni might be quite natural if we take into account the custom according to which, more often than not, the son of an artist learnt his father's craft in the latter's *bottega*, i.e. in his *atelier*. In fact, Jacopo's influence is also visible in the *Crucifixion* at Museo Correr dating from the same period as *St. Jerome and the Lion* (Birmingham, Barber Institute), a picture which everybody considered had been executed under the influence of Jacopo, about 1450. Jacopo's "gothicness" became less and less conspicuous though it was still present in the modulation of figures which, set against a perspectival background as in *Virgin and Child* (Paris, Fodor Collection), adopts a type of figurative representation which already characterizes the stage when Giovanni frees himself from the influence of his father and comes into contact with Donatello's and Mantegna's artistic achievements.

This "correction" of the line followed by Giovanni's art is no doubt connected with everything that occurred at the time in Venice and the neighbouring areas on the *terraferma*, when the new forms of figurative expression of the Renaissance were about to take root. Paolo Ucello had stayed in Venice between 1425 and 1430; in 1445 he went to Padua where he painted the *Titans* in the courtyard of the Vitaliani mansion. Beginning with July 1434 Filippo Lippi was present in Padua for a few years. He was still there when Masolino, on his way back from Hungary, stopped in Padua for a short stay. In 1443, Donatello arrived in Padua where, for 10 years running, he worked busily on the commissions he was given. A year before, in 1442, Andrea del Castagno had started painting a fresco in the church of San Zaccaria in Venice; the figures in it, executed in the manner of Massaccio, attracted the attention of the local artists, still under the influence of the Gothic means of expression and stimulated in their thorough study by the brief stay in Venice of Gentile da Fabiano and Pisanello. These genuine artistic events did not fail to attract Jacopo Bellini, who, captivated at first by the art of Gentile da Fabriano — probably by the magnificent *Sea Battle Between the Venetians and Otto III*, destroyed in the fire that broke out in the Doge's Palace in 1577, — was to take a deep interest, later on, in the placing of figures in perspective landscapes. This feature is obvious not only in a work such as the *Annunciation* (Brescia, Sant'Alessandro Church) but also in the book of drawings, today at the Louvre. It has been fully demonstrated that Jacopo's drawings — among which there are studies after ancient works — played an important role in the Venetian painting of the second half of the 15th. century [1]. On the other hand, it is a well known fact that in the testament he made on the 18th of February 1506, it was stipulated that Gentile made over to Giovanni his book of drawings, in compensation for the completion of the canvas depicting *St. Mark Preaching in Alexandria*. The stipulation has undoubtedly more than a sentimental value: it is quite telling for the manner in which the artistic concepts and the figurative models as such were handed down from generation to generation and carefully preserved as valuable possessions.

Meanwhile Andrea Mantegna, a painter who was to play a decisive role in the evolution of Venetian painting, was trained in the workshop of Squarcione (1397 — c. 1474) in Padua. Born in 1431, he was working independently in 1448 when he was commissioned to decorate, together with Niccolò Pizzolo, half of the Ovetari Chapel; the other half was to be painted by Antonio Vivarini and his brother-in-law Giovanni d'Alemagna. When the latter died in 1450 Antonio Vivarini gave up working in the Ovetari Chapel and went back to Venice. However, Mantegna went on working until 1455, a period of time in which his style was to crystallize rapidly, becoming more and more strikingly accurate and sculptural — characteristic features that combined in a masterly way in the altar dedicated to San Zeno (1456—1459) in the church by the same name in Verona. The link between Giovanni Bellini's earlier works and Mantegna's artistic creation is beyond any doubt the result of the direct contacts between the two artists who, in 1453, had become very close as Mantegna had married his sister. The influence Mantegna's art exerted upon Venetian painting marked the appearance within the latter of a differentiation of its formal structures. Critics have established the fact that, if for Jacopo Bellini and for Antonio Vivarini the appearance of Mantegna on the firmament of art "was the paradigm of a yet unattainable modernism, for Giovanni Bellini, as well as for Bartolomeo Vivarini and many others it was a reference point which could not be ignored." [2] Reformulating the lesson of Mantegna's painting in which stress was laid on determining plastic form, Giovanni Bellini sought from the very beginning to interpret in a less cold and less archaeological manner, without rendering absolute the tendency of emphasizing volumes. Mantegna's dramatism and plasticity undergo a metamorphosis in a pictorial sense, and the reminiscences of the chromatics in the works of Jacopo Bellini or Antonio Vivarini are still vivid. This brilliant palette, with its bright tones, is also influenced by the tradition of the Venitian mosaics. Bellini's sensitiveness itself enhances the pathos of the Paduan master by means of a warm colour scheme; thus his plastic language changes in the Venitian sense and determines, on the other hand, a reinterpretation of the themes treated by Mantegna. The *Crucifixion* (Milan, Museo Poldi Pezzoli), one of Bellini's early works, is proof of it. [3] The face of the donor in this picture recalls that of the donor in *St. Ursula and Her Companions* (Venice, Gallerie dell'Accademia), a genuine stylistic replica of the painting on the same subject executed a few years before by Antonio Vivarini for the church of San Pietro in Oliveto (Brescia). The composition shows the painter's concern with monumentality despite the small dimensions of the picture; the colour palette resembles Mantegna's vigorous chromatism, brick-red and yellow are predominant. The abandoning of the modes of expression of Jacopo Bellini and Antonio Vivarini in *The Crucifixion* (Poldi Pezzoli collection) is the natural consequence of an evolution in the conception of representation, an evolution already visible — in milder forms — in *St. Ursula and Her Companions*. The landscape in *The*

Crucifixion mentioned above, drawn in perspective, has its source of inspiration in the Ovetari chapel (the backgrounds), evincing also a concern with details, with the detail very much like the care for minutiae of miniature painters. It is interesting to draw a comparison between this work and two others with the same inconography. In the *Crucifixion* at the Civico Museo Correr (Venice) — which was made a little later than the similar work in the Poldi Pezzoli Museum — Mantegna's influence is visible in the treatment of the landscape forming the background. The firm precise construction of the landscape — based on a carefully studied gradation of the planes — the flow of a large sluggish river flanked by roads that lose themselves among the hills modelled with respect for an optic illusion deriving from the close study of reality — proves that the painter had acquired full mastery of the new modes of representation typical of the Renaissance. Here the figures are more strikingly outlined, and Mantegna's classicism is visible both in the groups in the second plane and in the whole organization of the composition. However, the work possesses the features characteristic of Giovanni's art; the vast space and broad setting, the spacious landscape are supported by a subtler yet energetic brushwork trying to set off some luminous zones able to make the on-looker participate in the drama unfolding in the landscape. All the critical works dealing with Giovanni Bellini's art have always laid stress — and with good reason too — on the fact that, though Mantegnesque in the organization of the space, it evinces the painter's keen insight into the real. The hills, waters, bridges, trees are those peculiar to the hilly region of Venezia. *The Crucifixion* at the Civico Museo Correr has been almost unanimously dated between 1455 and 1460, a period of time when Mantegna was in Venice. Grasping with good reason the link between this work and *The Agony in the Garden* (London, National Gallery) all specialists date the latter work about 1459—1460, a period of time when Mantegna executed a painting on a similar subject, today in London, at the National Gallery. The relationship between these works also poses the problem of the interaction between the work of the two artists. Bellini's version of *The Agony in the Garden* is characterized by the broadly irradiating chromatics which soften the firm, incisive line and contours. Similar features are also characteristic of the *Crucifixion* at the Museo Correr. A similar display of colour is to be found in the *Transfiguration* (Venice, Civico Museo Correr) which the same as *The Agony* . . . had been attributed to Mantegna until the end of the 19th century. The three personages, bathed in crepuscular light, are silhouetted against the horizon. The melancholy atmosphere is enhanced, like in *The Agony* . . ., by the barren rock-bound landscape in the foreground, jarring as it were with the nostalgic hills that lose themselves in the distance towards the sides of the picture. *The Transfiguration* is also dated 1455—1460. In this period Bellini does not oppose to Mantegna's vision — a vision of his own, but a personal poetics which was to become ever more profound. In the *Crucifixion* at the Museo Civico (Pesaro), which can be dated between 1455 and 1460, we can distinguish, besides the obvious influence of Jacopo Bellini and of Mantegna — in the treatment of the face more especially —, a northern element coming from the painting of Rogier van der Weyden. However, the specific orientation of Giovanni Bellini's art, based on the direct study of nature, of the relations between objects and light will prevail, evincing a tendency towards softening the rigidity of forms, in contrast with his father's art and also with the experience of the Paduan school (which derives in fact from the Florentine school). Giovanni Bellini's realism does not possess the harshness, the sternness the Paduan school promoted. At the end of the 19th. century, Cavalcaselle and Crowe noted (in the monograph devoted to Titian) that a thorough study of Classicism, as well as the difficult and subtle problems of linear perspective Mantegna was so eager to know, were of interest to Giovanni only if they did not go against his interest in colour which, at the time, helped define the main lines of force of his art. R. Longhi, in a particularly important essay on Venetian painting [4], pointed out that Giovanni tended to modify Mantegna's statuesque images by dilating the planes and by less vigorous contours. "The sense of the bas-relief," writes Longhi, "was the utmost result an artist like Giovanni Bellini, still in the orbit of Mantegna, could attain . . ."

We do not wish that the lines above should create the impression that we want to overemphasize the dependence of Giovanni's early career on his brother-in-law. But things were actually different: the attempt to escape the seduction exerted by the striking images conceived by Mantegna, the assimilation of Donatello's experience and of Piero della Francesca's lesson as well — by trying to fuse the elements of the real, in the famous perspectival synthesis between form and colour — reveal the germs of the subsequent evolution of Giovanni's painting.

Generally speaking Giovanni Bellini's experience reflects the stylistic dilemma of the entire Venetian painting in the latter half of the 15th. century.

We should perhaps dwell, in passing at least, on the possible relationships between Giovanni's art and that of Donatello. By common consent, the critics consider the *Pietà — Christ Dead Supported by Two Angels* (Venice, Civico Museo Correr) to have derived iconographically from Donatello's bas-relief for the altar in the Church of San Antonio. Christ's livid body, the colour of ivory, supported by two angels bearing the typical stamp of Donatello, is stylistically related to a work on the same subject housed by the Accademia Carrara in Bergamo, which everybody has dated 1455. In both cases the reference to Donatello's bas-reliefs is absolutely necessary. In the latter work the forms are less evolved and the painting, on the whole, seems less influenced by the technical novelties that appeared in the middle of the century, outside the Venetian artistic milieu. In the *Pietà — Dead Christ* (Museo Poldi Pezzoli, Milan) generally dated between 1464 and 1468, the manner in which the figure is set in the sharply delineated landscape, the unity of feeling between all the planes, impart coherence to the image. The utter solitude of the figure silhouetted against the golden sky at twilight heightens the dramatic character of the scene and suggests, at the same time, a link with northern art. The same pathetic note can be traced in *Christ Wounded Blessing* (Louvre), which critics always compare with the triptych by Rogier Van der Weyden in the same museum. [5]

At the time when Bellini was working on the painting today in Paris — about 1460 according to most research workers — there are no signs of the presence of works by Van der Weyden in Venice. Giovanni Bellini may have seen them in Ferrara. But the influence of Donatello, limited in these works to some aspects of the *découpage*, proportions and dynamics of the figures, is quite visible in the Virgin and Child executed during Giovanni Bellini's youth. The painter repeatedly treated the same subject all along his artistic career leaving a large number of variants. In *Virgin and Child* (Civico Museo Malaspina, Pavia) — in which a feeling for colour prevails, inherited from the Neo-Byzantine traditions which his father's work echoed — there is an incipient tendency towards monumental figures. In all probability this is the period of time stretching from 1455 to 1460. The *Madonna Davis* (New York, Metropolitan Museum of Art) seems to have been painted later, as it is superior in point of form: the classical monumentality of the figure of the Virgin is also heightened by the simpler drapery of the cloak. The landscape behind the figures — though influenced by Mantegna — possesses a typically Bellinesque sweetness treated as it is with a sweeping colour freedom. Both the portrait of the Virgin and the face of the Child are the natural development of the types in the picture belonging to the Fodor collection (Paris) dated by Longhi about 1460. The *Kessler Madonna* (Amsterdam,

Rijksmuseum), attributed to Giovanni, represents a synthesis of his artistic experience enriched by the contact with the works of Donatello and Mantegna. And yet, in spite of the specific filtering of colour and of the gradually subdued light as it reaches the horizon, his authorship is not quite sure. The powerful plastic features of the Child's face recalls the similar work at the Staatliche Museen (Berlin-Dahlem). A massive contribution of his apprentices is quite possible in both works dated soon after 1460, as suggested by the stylistic correspondences with the *Virgin and Child Blessing* (in the former Lehman collection, New York) where the play of volumes is enhanced by the strongly marked lines of contours of the figures. In the early 1460 Giovanni Bellini completed a number of works on the same subject. The respective dates have not been — they could hardly have been — established by critics as their arguments do not rest on conclusive sources, but on their attempt to place them — temporally — within a typological series in which the intermediate links have not been discovered. Things become even more complicated owing to the difference of opinions concerning the authenticity of some paintings. The best known are, undoubtedly, the *Madonna Trivulzio* (Milan, Civiche Raccolte d'Arte) and the *Madonna Greca* (Milan, Brera). In the former work more specially — which specialists dated between 1460 and 1470 — we are impressed by the precision and accuracy of the drawing, the noble features of the Virgin — serene and melancholy —, and by the rich attire. It is the personages in the *Madonna Greca* that seem to be silhouetted against a golden background, reminiscent of the Byzantine conception. The sculptural featuring of the Child is typically Donatellian. The two works could be dated even earlier, about 1460, if we take into account the lack of any rudiments of a landscape as well as their general "primitive" aspect.

However, the most interesting works of the period when such important elements melt in the art of Bellini to form an organic whole, are *The Blood of the Redeemer* (National Gallery, London) and *Pietà, with the Virgin and St. John.*

The iconography of the former recurs seldom and it was studied in detail by Erwin Panofsky [6], in his youth. There is a striking resemblance between Giovanni's painting and Crivelli's work, today at the Poldi Pezzoli Museum, whose source of inspiration is the same. The monumentality of Christ's figure is probably due to a thorough study of ancient sculpture. On the parapet separating the pavement (seen in perspective) from the landscape in the background two scenes are visible, one of which only representing to all appearances a pagan sacrifice. The separation of the foreground from the background by a parapet anticipates to a certain extent the manner in which the landscape was to be set in the picture, the way it appears in *Pala of Pesaro*. It is worth mentioning that this work together with the famous *Pietà* in the Brera testifies to complete shaping, in point of iconography and style, of a personal vision and manner of painting, the result of the integration and estimation of various experiences. The artist preserved the elements which made it possible to organize the composition in keeping with the new spatial figurative conception of the Renaissance, harmonizing forms and colours in a typically Venetian manner. The Paduan means of expression — still visible in the *Pietà* at Brera in the incised modelling of the figures — is counterbalanced here by the suggestive force of the palette which bestows on the characters an air of majestic sobriety.

It is the power to harmonize a rich colour palette — whose perfect mastery is due to the rich tradition of Venetian art — with the innovating spatial experiences of the time which explains the novelty Giovanni Bellini's early work brings into the Italian artistic landscape of the Quattrocento.

It is a fact that the freedom from the Mantegnesque models in the period from 1454 to 1460 was rather relative. We know for sure that, in the case of the *Presentation in the Temple*, (Venice, Galleria Querini Stampaglia) at least, Giovanni Bellini copied his brother-in-law *ad literam*. Indeed, in Mantegna's *Presentation in the Temple* (Berlin-Dahlem, Staatliche Museen) stated about 1454, the central group of personages is identical to those in Giovanni Bellini's painting. The figure in the second plane, on the right, may in all probability be Mantegna's self-portrait, the old man in the centre is Jacopo Bellini, while the young lady behind the Virgin Mary is Niccolosia, the sister of the Bellini brothers. In his own painting, Giovanni is supposed to have

Pietà (drawing)

added the portrait of his mother, on the left, substituting Gentile for Mantegna's self-portrait and adding his self-portrait on the right. The young faces of the two Bellini brothers point to a date of execution quite close to Mantegna's work. No doubt, the adoption of the whole subject and of its figurative elements in the *Presentation in the Temple* is an exception in Giovanni's work. In fact, numerous experts have expressed their doubts on the authenticity of this work. Anyway, even if the above painting is considered a stylistic exercise executed around 1460, i.e. before the triptychs in Santa Maria della Carità, this does not diminish the importance of that moment in the crystallizing of the major coordinates of Giovanni's painting. The triptychs in Santa Maria della Carità as well as the polyptych dedicated to San Vicenzo Ferreri in the Venetian Church of Santi Giovanni e Paolo possesses stylistic elements which are a logical consequence of elements discernible in *The Blood of the Redeemer* and in the *Pietà* in the Brera. Thus, there is a striking resemblance between Donatello's angel (the symbol of St. Mathew) in the Paduan church and the announcing angel in the polyptych dedicated to San Vincenzo Ferreri. A comparison between the figure of John the Baptist in the triptych dedicated to St. Sebastian in Santa Maria della Carità and Donatello's statue in Santa Maria Gloriosa dei Frari is illustrative thereof. The stylistic influence of Donatello's altarpiece in Padua is also visible in Giovanni's treatment of the anatomy and in the arrangement of the folds of St. Christopher's mantle in the polyptych of San Vincenzo Ferreri. The figure of Christ, supported by angels, in the latter work, strikingly resembles the one in the *Pietà* of the Brera.

We shall not dwell on the triptychs in the Church of Santa Maria della Carità (today in the Galleria dell'Accademia): specialists are not unanimous in ascribing them to Giovanni. At first they were considered to have belonged to Vivarini's school. Berenson — who was of this opinion only until 1913 [7] — was followed by all the critics who embraced his opinion that the polyptychs belonged to Giovanni's school. Giovanni may have executed only certain parts, hard to trace owing to successive restorations.

An important stage in Bellini's art is clearly illustrated by the *Polyptych of San Vincenzo Ferreri*. To the heightening of the monumentality of the figures is added here the powerful and luminous irradiation of colour spread over large surfaces. In the big panels, the human figures, which are the centres of attraction in point of colour, stand out in bold relief against the background drawn in perspective and acquire plastic independence. When examining the *predella* there was also much debate on the scenes representing the "miracles" attributed to San Vincenzo Ferreri: the rescuing of a drowned man and the resurrection of those buried under ruins, the resurrecting of two dead people, that of a child and the liberation of a prisoner. When analysed stylistically, the *predella* appears to be older than the one describing *The Story of Drusiana*, the only part of a *predella* — executed between 1468 and 1471 — dedicated to St. John the Baptist, formerly in Santa Maria della Carità in Venice, today in the collection of Prince Ruprecht of Bavaria (in the Lentstetten Castle). If we admit that *The Story of Drusiana* is by the hand of Giovanni, it follows that the *predella* describing the miracles wrought by San Vincenzo Ferreri is by the same hand. [8]

We believe that it was during that time that Giambellino came into contact with the art of Piero della Francesca. It is quite probable that his attempt at imparting a new significance to space by using architectural elements as firm points of reference, was inspired, to a certain extent, by Piero's art. A comparison between the *Flagellation* at Urbino, dated by Longhi about the middle of the century [9], and the last compartment on the right of the predella in the polyptych of San Vincenzo by Giovanni Bellini — a compartement in which the arrangement of the figure in space somehow recalls Piero's respective work — helps us clearly detect the awkward plastic organization of the image in the latter work. The very appearance of the Saint as liberator seems discordant in the scene in which the landscape with a tower is typically Bellinian. Revealing a surer hand in point of composition, the *predella* depicting *The Story of Drusiana* evinces a particular sense of balance in the image, achieved by grouping the figures in such a way as to be in unison with the architectural backgrounds. Most likely, it was during that time, about 1470, that Giovanni came to know directly, after his journey to Pesaro, the various ways in which space was organized in central Italy by the school of Piero. It was the moment when he executed the altar for the Church of San Francesco, in Pesaro, the capital work of his mature period of artistic creation. It represents an acme in Bellini's endeavours to combine the incisive lines and the *chiaroscuro*, derived from the experience of the Paduan school, with the Venetian colour harmony made to accord with the synthesis between form and colour, Piero della Francesca had achieved. It is now that the new conception of the relationship between space and colour fully comes to the fore in Giovanni's work. There are no documents recording a journey to Pesaro, but there is no doubt whatever that he visited his mother's birthplace. Critics have discussed at length this problem, essential in establishing the chronology of Bellini's work as well as the time when they were executed in comparison with the works of Antonello da Messina. The presence of the latter in Venice is attested in 1475 and his name is, as a rule, connected with the generalization of oil painting, a

13

technique which before him had been used only sporadically in the Venetian area. We have seen that Bellini's experiments in the field of perspective were on no account determined by the art of Antonello, who had come to Venice after he had assimilated the experience of Piero. As the altarpiece in Pesaro was executed in oil technique, it is easy to understand the interest of research workers in establishing plausible dates for Giovanni's work. It was only in the past few decades that critics became more and more positive in establishing that the work was painted about 1470—1471. The hypothesis was put forward by Palluchini [10] who found that the other part of the *Coronation of the Virgin* appears on the retable (dated 1471) by Marco Zoppo, formerly kept in Berlin and then destroyed. As Giovanni's work could not have been made before that year, it was quite logical to conclude that it was executed between 1470 and 1471, an interval which, as early as 1914, seemed to Longhi to be a term *ante quem*.

The changes in Bellini's artistic means of expression, which the Pesaro altarpiece evince, do not regard the type of composition only, a type characterized by his attempt to heighten the perspectival illusion. There is supreme freedom in the use of the colour palette. Liberated from the violent constraint of line, the painter grants particular attention to chromatic effects. Close tonalities are prevalent, lending more cohesion to the whole. The colours are all harmoniously blended by means of a flooding light which projects them against the background without setting them off — as it happened in most of his previous works. The central panel breathes to the full the atmosphere of "equilibrium between the human and the divine" which Fiocco mentioned in the monograph he wrote in 1960, in which he held, with good reason, that Giovanni Bellini must have led "the delicate and ordered Byzantine rhythm to the rational classicism of the Renaissance, spatial and corporal, steeped it in an atmosphere of human gentleness, whose secret lies (...) in the golden light of a divine earthly day." [11]

As far as we are concerned, we cannot help noticing the landscape, first and foremost, which helps the scene in the central panel suggest spaciousness. The precise geometry of the fortifications on the hill stands out against a sky where thin clouds are floating, illuminated by the still glimmering twilight. Whoever stops to look at the skies in Giovanni Bellini's paintings is bound to notice the rich hues, the subtle colour gradations varying according to the time of day. In his early paintings, Giovanni had already sought to render carefully the diaphanous tints in the distance, the division of the sky into zones which are often reddish in the lower part, a colour which grows paler and paler to reach the zones painted gray on which the luminous clouds projected against the intense blue all around are floating. It is obvious that in his landscapes Giovanni was trying in fact to intensify the emotion direct observation produced, for in many cases they have been identified. The fortification rising in the background of the central panel of the painting was supposed to represent the castle of Gradara conquered in 1463 from the city of Rimini by Alessandro Sforza, "signor" of the city of Pesaro. Comparing the architectures painted with those existing in the respective epoch, recent studies have identified the fortress in the panel at the base of the pilasters on the right as the fortress of Costanza, which the famous architect Laurana had started building about 1434. If we accept this hypothesis, the altarpiece in Pesaro should be placed in the second half of the 1470's; thus the arrival of Antonello da Messina in Venice should be viewed in its many possible implications.

What is in fact the significance of Antonello's coming to the city of the doges?

As is known, in painting on wood panels the water colours with egg-yolk to bind them are spread in a thin layer on a ground or priming. In time tempera changes into a shining surface covered by a network of cracks. At first the use of drying oils did not discard tempera altogether, a technique which made it possible to preserve the transparency of colours. Drying oils made colours too thick; that is why the painters found it necessary to dilute the colours with resins. Oil painting enabled painters to use a wider range of tones and to pass more easily from a shade to another, from a chromatic zone to another, which made it possible to achieve a subtler difference of planes. Giovanni Bellini, like most of the Italian painters of the time, did not give up some mixed techniques, not even after Antonello came to Venice. It was only in the last years of the 15th. century that he was to use mostly oil painting (before this period techniques were difficult to identify).

When Antonello was preparing to come to Venice, Giovanni was making the portrait of Jörg Fugger, in oil on wood panel. The painting is dated 1474, the year when the German banker is known for sure to have been in Venice. During the same period, Giovanni painted his remarkable *Pietà*, today in the art gallery in Rimini; but this time he used tempera on a wood panel. The dark background against which the figures stand out in both paintings recalls Antonello's portraits, though this could also be the result of his contact with similar models. The absence of perspective is unusual, especially when we think that only a few years before — in the *Coronation of the Virgin* as well as in the panels of the *predella* in the Pesaro altarpiece the scenes are set in open spaces. The emotional intensity in each scene is determined by the direct participation of the whole natural setting in the crystallization of a particular mood. The bare landscape in the panel describing the fight of St. George with the dragon, for instance, is rendered human only by the inexpressive prayer of the prisoner and by the solitary presence of the crenellated tower of the citadel. In like manner there is a feeling of utter loneliness in the square dominated by the slender figure of St. Terentianus, behind whom through the arch of the gate we can see the space guarded by the famous *comignoli* — the chimneys of the Venetian houses.

It is obvious that the presence or absence of the elements of perspective cannot supply any positive information on the inner evolution of Giovanni's painting; neither can the dark backgrounds suggest with any degree of certainty the particular moment when he became acquainted with Antonello's painting. Towards the middle of the 1470's the master went on painting his favourite themes, the long series of *Virgin and Child*, so close to one another iconographically that they can almost be considered the obsessive leit-motif of his entire work. This is the period when Bellini executed *Saint Justine* (Milan, Bagatti Valsecchi Collection) whose serene, dreamy, but at the same time peaceful and mysterious beauty we shall meet again in most of the Virgins in the next period, beginning with *Virgin Enthroned Adoring the Child Asleep* (Venice, Gallerie dell'Accademia). The same transparence of the air where diaphanous clouds floated, the same studied arrangement of the robes in large folds, each following a precise direction without thereby making the figures rigid, the same expression suggesting a murmured prayer, or thoughts rising above the things below, the same discrete emphasis of the anatomy of forms, bring the work in the Bagatti Valsecchi Collection close to the *Virgin and Child* at the Accademia dei Concordi in Rovigo, to the similar work to be found at the Museo di Castelvecchio in Verona, and to the *Virgin Adoring the Child Asleep* in the Contini-Bonacossi Collection, in Florence.

However, if we can state precisely that the Madonnas belonging to the interval between 1475 and 1480 are the logical result of the painter's entire previous artistic creation, the portraits — of precise or doubtful authorship — dating from the same period are not. Quite significantly, they have often been mentioned in connection with Antonello's work, though they are included in all the catalogues listing Giovanni Bellini's works. Carpaccio's name was mentioned, with good reason, in connection with *Portrait of a Youth* (Accademia Carrara, Bergamo) as well as with *Portrait of a Woman* (Rijksmuseum, Amsterdam).

The *Portrait of a Humanist* (Milan, Civiche Raccolte d'Arte) had been attributed to Antonello, then to Bellini; the same happened to the splendid *Portrait of a Youth* (Barber Institute, Birmingham), a work of a stirring beauty, instinct with a noble, secret melancholy, which recalls the angels in the *Pietà* in Rimini.

It seems to us that not even the analysis of the possible relations between the works by the two masters could dispel the confusion existing today in estimating the relations between Giovanni Bellini and Antonello, a confusion which was generated by the attribution of the portraits already mentioned. The study for the background of Giovanni Bellini's predella in the Church of Santi Giovani et Paolo—which Vasari regarded as "one of the best ever made" (in Venice — author's note) [12] — could have thrown some light on this much debated problem. It could be connected with the similar work made for the Church of San Cassino—of which only fragments have been preserved today at the Kunsthistorisches Museum in Vienna — famous at the time as shown in a letter Pietro Buono wrote to Galeazzo Sforza in 1476, in which he used the most laudatory terms about it.

Unfortunately Giovanni Bellini's work was destroyed in a conflagration in 1867; it can be seen today only in a bad enough photo of a copy — lost too — made in the 19th. century.

It seems that it is for the first time in his artistic career that, in this altarpiece Giovanni Bellini unified the space in which the *Sacra Conversazione* takes place by means of architecture, following thus in the steps of Piero della Francesca. Almost simultaneously and independently of Bellini, Antonello did the same in the retable for San Cassino. Bellini's contact with Piero's *Sacra Conversazione* (Milan, Brera) contributed no doubt to the elimination of the mediaeval patterns of the polyptychs in Giovanni's art, teaching him to organize perspective in architectural spaces. On the other hand, we should point out that Giovanni's use of perspective — even in the works depicting *Sacra Conversazione* — is not meant to mark the limits of space, to close it, but to dilate and extend it as far as the infinite, even if the opposite is also possible, as it is in *Pala di San Giobbe* (Venice, Gallerie dell'Accademia). Such tendency is the consequence of a new outlook on the relationships between man and nature, of the fact that the painter is aware that the individual is part and parcel of the cosmos within which he acts like a component of the whole. In fact, Giovanni Bellini is particularly interested in rendering the depth of space by means of the relation between colours. The elements of the landscape come to play a very important role, allowing more freedom in the treatment of figures, in the arrangement of groups, in the use of various shades of colour and of gradation. In *Resurrection* (Staatliche Museum Berlin-Dahlem) Jesus Christ rises in Majesty above the chains of hills dominated by the castle of Monselice, above the benumbed nature waiting for the invigorating breath of spring. One fresh morning light is preparing to bathe everything descending to the valleys between the bare hills.

Bellini evinces a tendency to give monumental dimensions to the various elements of the landscape, originating perhaps in his desire to adjust nature to the objects created by man. In his landscape the architecture created by man is set in contrast with the architecture of nature so expressively at times that it becomes harsh. The preservation of the graphic accents creates the impression of force the ambient milieu breathes, as it appears in *St. Jerome* (Florence, Contini-Bonacossi Collection). We should dwell a little longer on the symbiosis between the architectural monuments in the background which belong to different styles and epochs, as this is not the only time such a feature appears in the work of the great Venetian painter. Beside the fortress built in the Romanesque style peculiar to the North of Italy, there appear

Augustus' bridge in Rimini and the funeral monument of Theodoric in Ravenna. The visual synthesis characteristic of Bellini's landscapes is also emphasized, we believe, by this symbiosis.

The graphic accents we were referring to above, which he used in order to stress the wild grandeur of nature, reappear in *St. Francis in Ecstasy* (New York, Frick collection) which the critics praised so enthusiastically that it came to be regarded as "one of the finest paintings of the Quattrocento". [13] The iconographic solution is not the usual one: the image of the person who impresses the stigmata is absent from the picture; his presence is only suggested by a strong luminosity of the sky as well as by the ecstatic attitude of the saint waiting with outstretched arms for the miracle to happen. The details of the landscape, worthy of the Flemish painters in their minute reconstitution, are those of an everyday scene, bucolic we might say. *St. Francis in Ecstasy*, with all its component parts so perfectly knit together, is certainly the fruit of the artist's mature years. The coherence of the image is determined by the permeating quality of the light, which enhances the chromatic value of the landscape.

The Transfiguration, (Naples, Galleria Nazionale di Capodimonte) is a very significant work for Giovanni Bellini's later orientation. The three apostles are looking in amazement at the personage who has suddenly appeared in front of them; they withdraw with a gesture of defence in the face of his blinding brilliance. All the virtues present in Bellini's earlier works concerning the achievement of a real synthesis between spatial freedom and colour are brilliantly confirmed in the *Transfiguration*, though the stress is not shifted, not even partly, on the naturalistic treatment of the image. A warm, subdued light comes from below the horizon sending its rays in the direction of the onlooker, withdrawing behind the objects after a last effort to envelop them. Recent restorations have revealed that the leaves of the trees on the right were added later, in the 16th. century. The heads of Peter and James too have been touched up, while the little man on the right, in the middle ground, who is talking with the personage clad in oriental attire, is a later addition. Here, the same as in other works, the landscape blends into one single image various reminiscences, details that indirectly bring to mind the humanistic culture of the time, such as Theodoric's grave and the steeple of the church of Saint Appolinare in Classe in Ravenna. This painting dating from the middle of the 1480's — a moment when the master was advanced in years — was followed soon after by a very large altarpiece (471×258 cm), formerly in the Venetian church of San Giobbe, representing the *Virgin and Child*, flanked by SS Francis, John the Baptist and Job on the left, by Damien, Sebastian and Louis of Toulouse on the right. The lesson in the rendering of space he had learnt from Piero della Francesca reached perfection, the painter being interested in the same problems as he was in the retable for the church of Santi Giovanni e Paolo, destroyed in 1867, which we have already mentioned. The time when the work was completed was not later than 1487, considering the fact that *De Venetae Urbis Situ* by Sabellico, in which it is mentioned was published between 1487 and 1489. The attempt at dating it earlier increases the confusion in the chronology of Bellini's work, debatable enough as it is. We should note the fact that *Pala di San Giobbe* evinces a marked stylistic independence. All the elements of the composition contribute to this strong impression. The very mosaic in the semi-calotte of the apse in front of which rises the throne of the Virgin is typically Venetian. The solemn figures, the rich colour scheme of the architectural background, as well as the graphic precision of the contours of the personages, are all the most intimate features of Giovanni's art. The amazing precision with which the order and the semi-cylindrical vault are rendered and the perfect mastery of perspective are quite striking. The musicality and harmony of both chromatic relationships and proportions in *Pala di San Giobbe* mark — we believe — more even than in the *Transfiguration*, an equilibrium of all the tendencies previously manifested in Giovanni's work, which had reached one of its culminating moments. In the triptych standing in Santa Maria Gloriosa dei Frari in Venice, signed and dated 1488, we trace again all the features which — as shown above — combined to secure for the background of the predella in the church of San Giobbe a place apart in Bellini's painting. The richly decorated frame — drawn to all appearances by the artist himself — powerfully suggests a triptych. Despite their comparative independence, the scenes separated by pilaster strips form a single unitary image. Between the pilaster strips and the architectural elements painted behind the lateral groups of characters — Augustine and Peter on the left and Paul and Benedict on the right — one can distinguish the landscape. The natural daylight penetrates through these small apertures filling the space between the architectural elements with a permanent vibration, lending brilliance to the red brocade lining the apse and making the mosaic of the semi-calotte glitter. Thus the image of the *Virgin and Child* becomes particularly striking, a feature enhanced by the vigorous forms and the garb arranged in wide folds. The red, blue, yellow and green colours in the lanscape are spread over large surfaces, stressing the monumental character of the figures, giving depth to the space which, as already noticed seems to suggest a section in a Lombard church.

There is the same monumental vision in *Sacra Conversazione* of Murano, known also as *Pala Barbarigo*, after the name of Doge Barbarigo. It is quite obvious that

Pagan Allegory

the work resembles the triptych in Santa Maria Gloriosa dei Frari, in the sense that new relationships between light and colour are established, able to heighten the impression of monumentality and to set off the details of the landscape, are established. Here too the characterizations of the portraits anticipate — like in *Pala di San Giobbe* or in the triptych of Santa Maria Gloriosa dei Frari — the art of the great Venetian painters of the following century, of Titian and Veronese. In fact, the serene harmony of the figures in *Pala di San Giobbe*, the same as in the innumerable portraits in the

18

period of his old age, make the art of Giovanni — whose classical character seems to derive from an inner tendency rather than from any strict observance of the rules of archaeology resulting from his sources and from a peculiar cultural attitude — be often compared to the art of Raphael. However, the differences between the two artists come out even more clearly from the fact that, while Giovanni's classicism is based on a sumptuous art, a ceremonial art, the Byzantine one — sublimated through the experiences of the Lombard and Venetian Gothic on which the artist grafted Tuscan elements that had reached him through the direct channel of Donatello and indirectly through Mantegna — Raphael could see, in Urbino, the classical models of Piero della Francesca and Bramante. The echoes of Piero's lesson penetrated deep into Giovanni Bellini's work too, which little by little acquired a "Venetian" character. There is a dialectic relationship between innovation and tradition in Giovanni's work, which enables his renewing experiences never to alter — in spite of his richer means of expression — the original fund of the Byzantine spirit underlying the figurative tradition in the lagoon, that constant feature which gave its peculiar dimension to the art of the Renaissance in Venice. Such a vision, both familiar to the Renaissance and deeply Venetian, is clearly visible in the *Pala Barbarigo*. The Doge and donor, supported with a protecting gesture by St. Mark, seems to be a figure stepping out of the much later canvases of Titian. The lanscape on the right, in fact the best preserved part of the canvas, is an obvious "self-quotation" taken as such from the central panel describing *The Coronation of the Virgin* in the retable in Pesaro.

Giovanni's effort to make more room for space in his paintings, without thereby limiting it to the rigid patterns of a scenography, makes of him one of the most imaginative painters of the 15th. century, always bent on interpreting the plastic values of the landscape. In this respect, the *Religious Allegory* (Uffizi) reveals the painter's same interest in space which was so obvious in the *Transfiguration* in Capodimonte; the allegory is surprisingly modern owing to the subtle, refined colour scheme which fully contributes to "stylizing" all the details of the landscape. This time, however, the relationship between the personages in the foreground and nature is not so easily established. Unfortunately, the iconography of the Scene is not elucidated satisfactorily, despite some obvious links with its humanistic culture of the time. It was thought that the subject represents the so-called "pilgrimage of the soul" inspired by the panel of Deguilleville [14]. A similar kind of refined symbolism was subsequently to appear in the work of Giorgione, to whom the painting was in fact attributed for a time. Extremely complex, it arrests attention especially by the manner in which the so different attitudes of the figures correspond to the complexity of the landscape. It was pointed out that the presence of the limpid surface of the water makes the representation atemporal, its reflexes dissolving significances as it were. It is a religious and a lay work at one and the same time, the fruit of both realistic observation and imagination nourished by the humanistic texts then in circulation, for in what other way could one interpret the mysterious presence of the centaur standing on the other bank in an attitude of meditative doubt?

It is also difficult to make out the iconography of the four small paintings housed by the Gallerie dell'Accademia, which at first decorated a piece of furniture. They must have been executed about 1490, a time when Giovanni evinced a marked interest in the rendering of landscape, very close to the date when the allegory at the Uffizi was made. There were also lengthy discussions on the symbolic representation of the four works. A thorough iconographic study reveals very interesting data regarding the culture of the epoch, the texts in circulation, the connection between them, etc. It was first believed that *Summa Virtus*, the fifth allegory belonging to the same series and representing a winged monster with a woman's face, blindfolded and its claws resting on two metal spheres, was the work of Giovanni Bellini. Yet Longhi eliminated it from the Bellinian *corpus*. [15]

We have not room enough to dwell at length on the problem, yet we should mention the fact that there are no unanimous viewpoints concerning the iconographic significance of the five works. Two fundamental studies offer different solutions. The woman in the boat, holding the globe supported by a cupid is a symbolic representation of *Fickle Destiny*, i.e. *Iconostancy*, rather than a simple image of Venus Genitrix. Bacchus in his triumphal car drawn by cupids is the symbol of *Sloth* as contrasted with the symbol of *Perseverance* represented by the armed soldier — Mars? — who is walking away; the naked woman holding the looking-glass in her hand is *Prudence*, not *Truth*; the man emerging from the shell and talking with the serpent is the impersonation of *Infamy*; *Summa Virtus* concentrates the symbol of *Moderation, Courage, Justice*. [16] If we follow the indications of another researcher, the first work represents *Destiny*, the second the opposition between Bacchus and Mars, i.e. between *Vice* and *Virtue*, the third *Wisdom* foreseeing the future, the fourth *Deceit* or false prophecy, the fifth *Truth*. [17] Gamba [18] saw in the second work an allegory of *Labour*, in the third *Destiny*, in the fourth *Slander*. What we consider essential is the fact that in all five works — admitting nevertheless that *Summa Virtus* too belonged to the same series — the search for some new solutions becomes apparent; they are one more evidence of the interest in tackling some refined iconographic themes, in the arrangement of figures, in the setting of the image.

Some of these preoccupations can also be seen in the large number of Virgins the artist painted in the last two decades of the century. The desire to dilate the compositions by underlining some elements of the landscape — sometimes excessively simplified — such as in *Madonna degli Alberelli* dated 1487 (Venice, Gallerie dell'Accademia) where the figures rendered in bold relief against the greenish background of the screen are flanked on both sides by fragments of a landscape dominated by the slim silhouettes of two cypresses. In the *Virgin and Child* at the Accademia Carrara in Bergamo (1487—1495) in which he starts a new manner of disposing the figures, the Child being seated on the Virgin's left knee, the details of the landscape are rendered with the precision required by the need to give correct dimensions to the never absent *vedute* of the fortresses in the far distance. As to attributions, there was seldom any general agreement, a fact which can also be applied to the works above. In this context we believe that mention should be made of a small *Sacra Conversazione* representing St. Paul and St. George (Venice, Gallerie dell'Accademia), with generous chromatics, in which the features of the personages recall Giorgione's beginnings.

Portrait painting holds a place apart, a very important one, in Bellini's artistic creation of the last two decades of the 15th. century. It has been pointed out that the incissive contours of the faces is the result of Bellini's contacts with Antonello's portraits. The prevailing feature is the monumentality of the persons whose portraits the artist made, seen as a rule in half-profile. Their sculptural quality is emphasized by the firm lines which stand out determinedly against the black background, as in the portrait of Jacopo Marcello, the Head of the Venetian army between 1482 and 1484 (Washington, National Gallery, Kress donation). Such effects are sometimes heightened by the lighter atmospheric backgrounds which, towards the end of the century, replaced the dark ones. Such are the *Portrait of a Young Senator* (1485—1490) in the Museo Civico, Padova, or the *Portrait of a Young Man* (about 1500) at the Capitolina Picture Gallery. At the beginning of the 16th. century, Bellini made the *Portrait of Doge Leonardo Loredan* (London, National Gallery) in which the vigorous colouring combines with the firm line and volumes so as to impart great expressivity to the

Doge's features, enhanced by the metallic reflexes of the mantle embroidered with vegetal ornaments, inlaid as it were by the hand of a master jeweller.

The only portrait attributed to Bellini, which has a landscape as background, is believed to represent the famous Venetian humanist *Pietro Bembo*, (Hampton Court, Royal Collection) the man who, in his *Rhymes* (published in Venice in 1535) was praising the art of his old friend in the following splendid lines:

> *O imagine mia celeste et pura;*
> *Che splendid più che'l sole a gli occhi miei,*
> *Et mi rassembri il volto di colei,*
> *Che scolpita ho nel cor con maggior cura,*
> *Credo che'l mio Bellin con la figura*
> *T'habbia dato il costume anche di lei.**

The landscape in the *Portrait of Bembo* already prefigures a peculiar feeling of dim melancholy so characteristic of Giorgione's earlier works. The latter's name was repeatedly mentioned in connection with a large canvas (400×263 cm) hanging to this day in the Church of Santa Corona in Vicenza. Critics imagined even a collaboration of the young Giorgione, limited to the painting of the angel, clad in red standing in the left hand corner of the picture. [19] The attempt at tracing Giorgione's influence in the landscape as well is — we believe — quite disputable, especially as there is no proof whatever that Giorgione was apprenticed to the old master, an apprenticeship which might have supported the hypothesis of his intervention. Some rigidity in the succession of the planes, the comparative lack of precision of the details, as well as the manner in which the anatomy of the bodies is treated, reveal that the hand of the artist has grown rather tired, a hand which had been trained to paint such compositions long before Giorgione won any fame. The virtuosity of the master is quite visible in the light effects: his inimitable skies growing blood-red towards dusk, are peopled by the same red cherubs which appear in the *Virgin* coming from the Scuola della Carità (Venice, Gallerie dell'Accademia). The problem of the relationship between Giovanni Bellini and Giorgione must be viewed very cautiously for it is hard to admit there existed any reviving influence and — why not use the term? — even a "shaping influence" upon a work which — covering such a long span of time — possessed all the premises necessary for any fresh meditation upon his own poetic art. We do not wish to deny that it was quite possible for young Giorgione's art to have had a stimulating influence upon the art of the reverred master — about whom Dürer, when passing through Venice, had respectfully said the following: "He is very old, but he is still the supreme painter" *(Er ist sehr alt und noch immer der beste in der Malerei)* — we only wish to make clear his true dimensions again, the way the artist deserved it. At the beginning of the 16th. century, Giovanni Bellini developed his art, starting from the foundations of his own experience. This is graphically shown by the *Sacra Conversazione* in the Church of San Zaccaria in Venice, painted in 1505 and for so many reasons connected with *Pala di San Giobbe*. It is true that it was now that the master who had reached the great age of seventy-five, had the opportunity to see the works of Giorgione, which had appeared like an invigorating breath in the artistic life of proud Venice. Nevertheless, the modulation of colour function of atmospheric factors and of the

---

* Oh, my celestial and pure image
  which, in my eyes, shines brighter than the sun,
  and you resemble the face of she,
  who is so deeply engraved in my heart.
  I believe that my Bellini, with her appearance,
  has also given you her character.

luminosity of the sky was not new to Bellini who had made use of it on other occasions as well. His work rediscovers now — and this seems to be, in our opinion, the main characteristic of the master's art, paradoxically enough stimulated by his old age and never overwhelmed by it — a new sense of monumentality, expressed in *The Ascension of the Virgin* (Murano, San Pietro Martire) and in a composition representing *St. Jerome between SS Christopher and Augustine* (Venice, San Giovanni Crisostomo), both made in 1513. The latter work more especially reveals the influence of Sebastiano del Piombo who, towards the end of the first decade of the 16th. century, bestowed a new monumental vigour on the characters in his compositions. A more precise assessment of the relationships with Giorgione, Sebastiano del Piombo and Titian cannot ignore the decisive role Giovanni's art played in directing this art along a well established path: the understanding of the relationships between objects through the perspective of chromatic relations.

The *Descent from the Cross* (Venice, Gallerie dell'Accademia), already mentioned by Boschini [20] as the work of Marconi, belongs to the same period. Anyhow, the contribution of the pupil seems to have been small enough. It is quite certain that this landscape is by the hand of Giovanni; the whole conception according to which its component parts are disposed so as to form a vast amphitheatre, pleads in favour of this opinion: there is the town with its towers, the fortress, the withered tree, the fig-tree with its few branches, the hare in a thicket. There is nothing picturesque in the landscape which seems to envelop in a protective way the act performed in the background, an act in which the personages take part with tragic resignation. To all appearances the canvas, which may be dated about 1515, could be one of the last works of Giambellino. It is placed at the end of a very long experience which lasted for years, and which — to use a suggestive phrase — does not lead to "blind alleys". The landscape acquires a new function in the Madonnas of this period too; they are represented together with the Child, or in *Sacra Conversazione*, or again in the already classical hypostasis of a *Pietà*. Early in the century, in a masterpiece such as *Virgin and Child, John the Baptist and a Woman Saint* (Venice, Gallerie dell'Accademia) the landscape, the onlooker catches sight of it between the silhouettes of the personages, appears again: the regular, essentialized forms of the houses in the port descending gently from the hills in the direction of the sea, are surprisingly modern and so is the rural landscape in *The Virgin of the Meadow* (about 1505?) — today in the National Gallery, London — in which the poesy of the image is so intense that it was rightly said that all through the respective period Giambellino lent a new meaning to this type of image, making it express a "rural sacredness". [21] Even when the prevailing feeling is tragical like in the famous *Pietà* in the Gallerie dell'Accademia created around 1505 — whose iconography recalls the northern tradition of the *Vesperbild* — the lyricism of the image is not diminished. Some monuments that appear in the town forming the background have been identified: the pre-Palladian Basilica, the dome of Vicenza and the sanctuary on Mount Berico are only some of them. Once more does Giovanni Bellini use elements from the surrounding world so as to render his landscapes concrete. The fact that the personages in the foreground are not in perfect harmony with the space is not due — in our opinion — to his hypothetical failing power of expression but to the deliberate intention of the painter. The dramatic character of the scene in the background is highlighted by the very fact that it is separated from the townscape whose geometry makes the composition look cold, an impression heightened by the grey tones of the sky too.

The opposite effect — of calm majestic abandonment filled with mysterious serenity, is achieved in *Virgin and Child Blessing* (Detroit, Institute of Art) and also in the canvas by the same name to be found in Milan (Brera Picture Gallery) —

is achieved by the same means, i.e. by separating the characters from the natural environment which breathes a warm humanity in all the facets. Both the composition of the earlier work (dated 1509) and in the latter (probably 1510) are always connected with the poetic vision of Giorgione who died in 1510. The painting of the Brera distinguishes itself by an extremely refined colour scheme; the reddish flesh tint of the Virgin stands in contrast with the nacreous body of the infant whose expression is identified by the vividness of the eyes. A plain dotted with a few trees, autumnal stubble fields spread as far as the tall hills dominated by defence towers and houses over which rises a sky of a mat blue fretted with whitish clouds which a refreshing noonday rain has not dispersed. When looking at the face of the Madonna we cannot help comparing it to some images in Titian's pictures. The serenity, calm and equilibrium present in the old master's painting matches the springlike breath in the Venetian work of Giorgione and Titian! However, the problem of the connections between the art of Bellini and that of Titian is far more complex as is the evolution of the critics' opinions regarding a well-known work, *The Feast of the Gods* (Washington, National Gallery of Art, Widener donation), will illustrate it tellingly enough. The painting was made for Alfonso I d'Este's "camerino d'alabastro" in the Castle of Ferrara. As shown above [22], the work, meant at first for Isabella d'Este, was started in 1506. It took Bellini eight years to paint it. A first intervention over the initial painting seems to have occurred when the canvas was still in the painter's workshop: a landscape with shrubs, a bridge and a tower [23] were added on the left, all in Titian's manner. The painting was touched up for the last time by Titian again, when the famous "camerino" was rearranged. It was quite natural that he should be entrusted with the job, for he was familiar with the painting of the great master. Titian is said to have touched up the breasts of the nymphs, removing the clothes and making the picture look profane as the subject called for. The landscape too was altered to make it harmonize with the landscapes in other paintings meant for the same room of the castle. [24] It is a fact — and this brings us to the heart of the matter — that the effect of all Titian's additions was not to destroy the vision of the master but to interpret it, with all the required changes, from a "modern" stand. In other words Bellini's art resisted any attempt at renewing it, even if this renewal started from its innermost nature. As a matter of fact the respective work had a very interesting fate. Carried to Rome in 1598, to the Aldrobandini villa, it was seen there and copied by Poussin, contributing to the defining of the French master's style and entering — through his work — the modern figurative heritage.

The *Feast of the Gods*, deriving from *Orpheus* (Washington, National Gallery of Art) in point of theme, as well as *Nude with Mirror (Toilet of Venus* — Vienna, Kunsthistorisches Museum) and *The Drunkenness of Noah* (Besançon, Musée des Beaux-Arts) all of them made in the 1520's, are Giovanni Bellini's swan song. Based on some substantial modifications and on a considerable enrichment of humanist culture, the painting of the old master can still keep pace with the art of the young Giorgione and Titian. The great *teleri*, the large canvases he made for the Palazzo Ducale at different times and on various occasions, perished in the conflagration of 1577 and one aspect at least of his contribution, the one concerning his being a painter of "stories", is not known; we cannot, therefore, assess the share of his "inventions" in the work of his successors, though it is a fact that Carpaccio was able to see them (as well as Gentile's paintings) and benefit by them. This loss, however, cannot prevent us from grasping the significance and importance of Giovanni Bellini's artistic creation within the Venetian art of the golden century of the Renaissance.

Concerned with humanizing the sacred, Giovanni Bellini endeavoured to place, in art too, the human being in the centre of things. His work is an example of the aspiration towards the anthropocentrization of the artistic universe, an aspiration which had numerous points of contact with the broader movement of ideas, of philosophical debates, that developed all along those years. He is a typical representative of a time when the modification of the mind's structures obliged art to reassess its possibilities of expression, when the novelties in the field of technique — connected with the ever more serious study of perspective and with the use on a large scale of oil painting — became the reflex of a radically changed outlook of representation.

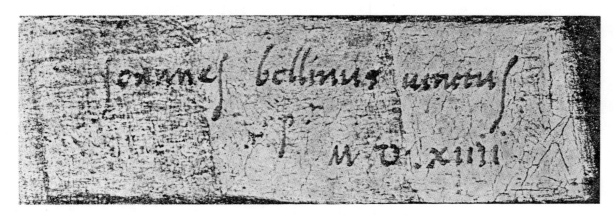

Bellini's Signature

That is why the contact between Giovanni's creation and that of his great contemporaries is not — when considered from a historical viewpoint — a proof of his weakness. It can be viewed as a permanent aspiration towards and concern with reinterpreting the problems of the work of art and with reconsidering its peculiar means of representation. The secret of the refreshing character of Giovanni's art lies in his ability to filter the data of the real through a sensitivity which was always awake, through an always vivid and active artistic thinking, eager to follow the teachings of the dialogues between creators and the surrounding world.

The cultural and artistic experiences that enriched the stylistic register of his works in the last year of his life never affected the intimate fund of Giovanni's artistic creation, dominated by a permanent search for measure and equilibrium, for poesy and harmony. With Giovanni Bellini any change is the consequence of a continual reconsideration and intepretation of his own means of expression, which left untouched the deep, genuine lyricism of the image. The intimacy and mystery of his work, published by a figuartive culture that had its starting point in the Byzantine and the Gothic heritage, was to evolve gradually, smoothly and without any spectacular leaps, so as to reach the "classical moment" of Venetian painting he aspired after, which he also conditioned and determined. It is difficult to imagine how Venetian painting would have looked in the absence of Giovanni Bellini. Anyway, it is hard to believe that the art of Carpaccio, Giorgione and Titian could have found a more fertile fulcrum in the local tradition than in the experience of the elderly master. Of course, the progress of the stylistic evolution of Venetian art would not have been substantially changed. However, a gem would have been absent from it, a gem whose flashes enhanced the brilliance of other precious stones. No doubt, the fraternity between people and things, which the work of the master left after him as a spiritual testament to Venetian painting and through it to the European one, would have been absent. And so would have been the soft, nostalgic light in the midst of which people remember they are gods, and "gods" return modestly to their former condition: humble human beings yet bearing the sacred stamp of their right to beauty and eternity.

NOTES

1. See M. RÖTHLISBERGER, *Notes on the Drawing Books of Jacopo Bellini*, in "The Burlington Magazine", XCVIII, 1956.
2. R. PALLUCHINI, *Giovanni Bellini*, Milan, 1959, p. 14.
3. Formerly attributed to Niccolò da Foligno and then to Giovanni Bellini by Fiocco, *Un'anconetta primitiva di Giambellino*, in "Rassegna Marchigiana", 1922.
4. R. LONGHI, *Piero dei Franceschi e lo sviluppo della pittura veneziana*, "L'arte", 1914.
5. G. ROBERTSON, *The Earlier Work of Giovanni Bellini*, in "Journal of the Warburg and Courtauld Institutes", XXIII, 1960, p. 48.
6. *Imago Pietatis*, in *Festschrift M. J. Friedländer*, 1927, p. 261 et seqq.
7. *Les quatre triptiques bellinesques de l'église de la Carità à Venise*, in "Gazette des Beaux Arts", 1913, p. 191 et seqq.
8. U. B. SCHMIDT (*Francesco Bonsignori*, in "Münchner Jahrbuch der Bildenden Kunst", 1961, p. 110 et seqq.) tried to support the idea that the polyptych of St. John the Baptist was the work of Laurano Padovano, an artist belonging to the group of those who were supposed to have executed the triptychs for the same church.
9. For other hypotheses see G. ARBORE, *Piero della Francesca*, Bucharest, 1974, Note 23, p. 32.
10. *Op. cit.*, p. 137
11. G. FIOCCO, *Giovanni Bellini*, Milan, 1960.
12. *Le vite . . .*, 1568, Ed. Milanesi, Florence, 1878, III, p. 163.
13. See M. MEISS, *Giovanni Bellini's S. Francis*, New York, 1964, p. 13.
14. See G. LUDWIG, *Giovanni Bellinis sogenante Madonna am See in den Uffizien, eine religiöse Allegorie*, in "Jahrbuch der Preussischen Kunstsammlungen", 1902, p. 163.
15. Who attributed it to Previtali? See R. LONGHI, *Viatico per cinque secoli di pittura veneziana*, Florence, 1964.
16. G. LUDWIG, F. RINTELEN, *Venezianischer Hausrat zur Zeit der Renaissance: Restello, Spiegel und Toilettenutensilen in Venedig zur Zeit der Renaissance*, in "Italienische Forschungen", Berlin, 1906, p. 170 et seqq.
17. G. F. HARTLAUB, *Spiegelbilder der Giovanni Bellini*, in "Pantheon" 1942; see also PALLUCHINI, *op. cit.*, 1959, p. 146.
18. *Giovanni Bellini*, 1937, p. 121.
19. E. ARSLAN, *Catalogo delle cose d'arte e d'antichità d'Italia. Vicenza. Le chiese*, Rome, 1956, p. 66 et seqq.
20. *Le ricche miniere della pittura*, Venice, 1664, p. 467.
21. BOTTARI, *Giovanni Bellini*, 2 vols. Milan, 1963, II, p. 11
22. E. Wind, *Bellini's Feast of the Gods. A Study in Venetian Humanism*, Cambridge (Mass.), 1948, pp. 22—26.
23. See J. WALKER, *Bellini and Titian at Ferrara*, London, 1956, p. 28
24. See E. BATTISTI, *Mitologie per Alfonso d'Este*, in "Rinascimento e Barocco", Turin, 1960, p. 112 et seqq.

CHRONOLOGY

c. 1425   Birth of Giovanni Bellini, son of Jacopo Bellini and Anna Rinversi. Vasari *(Le vite . . . , 1568)* shows that the artist was 90 years old when he died in 1516. So Giovanni seems to have been older than Gentile, Jacopo's eldest legitimate son (born 1429). However, contemporary evidence shows that Gentile was older than Giovanni and consequently, he was born only after 1430, if the assumption that Gentile was the son still unborn mentioned in Anna Rinversi's testament, in 1429, proves true.

     The wording of the testament of 1471 of the same Anna Rinversi (in which Giovanni was not mentioned and everything was left to "Gentili et Nicolae filiis meis et dicti quondam magistri Jacobi — i.e. "to Gentile and Nicolosia, my children, and the late master Jacopo's") led to the supposition that Giovanni was Jacopo's natural son.

1443   *Donatello is in Padua. Almost at the same time (1442), Andrea del Castagno is in Venice where he paints in San Zaccaria's.*

1453   Nicolosia, Giovanni's sister, marries Andrea Mantegna.

1454   Giovanni Bellini witnesses an act for the notary Giovanni Moisis: *Ser Johannes filius magistri Jacobis Belini San Leonis.*

1460   Gattamelata donates to the Basilica of San Antonio the altarpiece representing the Calvary. The work (lost today) bore the following inscription: *Jacopi Bellini Veneti patris ac Gentilis et Ioannis natorum opus MCCCCLX.* ("Made by Jacopo Bellini of Venice and by his sons Gentile and Giovanni"). The inscription is mentioned in Valerio Polidoro's *Le religiose memorie . . . ,* Venice, 1590.

1460—1471   In this period the artist executes the four polyptychs which formerly were placed on the altars in the sides of the choir of the Church of Santa Maria della Carità. Having been removed in Napoleon's time, they are now reassembled in the *Gallerie dell'Accademia.* The dates of their execution roughly correspond to the dates when the respective chapels together with their altars were assigned to the families that undertook to have the paintings done. In 1460 the Chapels of St. Laurence and St. Sebastian were completed and so were the Chapel of the Nativity in 1462 and that of the Virgin and Child in 1464. The triptychs were consecrated in 1471 together with all the altars of the church. First attributed to the two Vivarini, the polyptychs were then possitively ascribed to Giovanni and his *atelier* by Berenson and Adolfo Venturi.

1464   Documents record the building of the altar dedicated to San Vicenzo. The polyptych, already attributed to Giovanni Bellini by Sansovino *(Venezia città nobilissima e singolare,* Venice, 1581) was executed later on.

     Ridolfi *(Le Maraviglie dell'arte . . . ,* Venice, 1648, van Handeln Publishers, Berlin, 1914) holds that Giovanni's name, together with the date — 1464 — could be read on one of the two paintings lost today, executed for the Scuola di San Gerolamo.

1470   Bellini is commissioned to paint a large canvas depicting *The Deluge and Noah's Ark* for the Scuola di San Marco. It is likely that the work was never executed, since, in 1482 Bartolomeo Montagna contracts with the Scuola to paint a canvas on the same subject.

     Death of Jacopo between January 7 and November 25. The last mention of the artist in life appears in a document dated January 7, while in his wife's testament dated November 25, Anna Rinversi is already identified as "widow".

1471   Elisabeta Morosini suggests to Marco Morosini that Gentile and Giovanni Bellini are the most suitable painters to teach "the practice of drawing to our Domenico" *(la rason del disegno a pre Domenego nostro).*

1473   On April 18, Antonio di Choradi writes from Pera to his brother-in-law Niccolò Gruetto asking him to purchase a Christ from Lazzaro Bastiani, and if Lazzaro is dead to apply to "Ziane bellino."

1474   The date of June 20, is inscribed on the back of the painting representing Jörg Füger, today in the Contini-Bonacossi Collection (Florence).

1479   August 28. There is talk of replacing Gentile — who was about to leave for Constantinople — by his brother Giovanni for the restoration of the paintings in the Sala del Maggior Consiglio in the Palazzo Ducale.

1480   *July 1.* Giovanni is charged with restoring and executing the paintings in the Sala del Maggior Consiglio. He is rewarded for it with the first vacant "senseria" (commission) at Fondaco dei Tedeschi and a special recompense of 80 ducati from the Ufficio del Sali, besides the refund of his expenses.

1482   *February 26.* The *Signoria* summons Giovanni to complete *The Sea Battle against Otto*, in the Palazzo Ducale (Sansovino, *op. cit.*, 1581).

1483   *February 26.* The College issues a decree exempting Giovanni from all obligations to the guild of painters (Fraglia dei Depintori) in order to enable him to devote all his energies to the work he was entrusted with. He is appointed "pittore del dominio" (official painter to the Republic).

         June 30. Gaspare Trissino makes provision in his will for a payment to Giovanni Bellini commissioned to paint a *Resurrection of Christ* for a chapel in the Vicenza Cathedral.

1484   "*Ser Zuane belin depentor*" joins the confraternity of the Scuola Grande di San Marco. He also belongs to the confraternity of the Scuola Grande della Misericordia.

1485   *July 30.* He solemnly guarantees the dowry of his wife Ginevra. At the same date they were living in the Santa Marina district.

1487   Signs and dates *Madonna degli alberelli.*

1488   July 8. Giovanni and Gentile ask Aloise Vivarini to paint a "teler" (a canvas) for the Sala del Maggiore Consiglio, *nel modo che lavorano al presente li do fratelli Bellini* (in the manner in which the two Bellini brothers are working at present).

1489   September 23. Ginevra, *uxor egregy viri ser Ioannis bellinj pictoris de confino sancte marina* — (the wife of the distinguished gentleman Ser Giovanni Bellini, painter ...) dictates his testament. She mentions in it their son Aloise, who in his turn, makes his will in 1498.

1490   Signs and dates *The Supper of Emaus* (destroyed now) for the family of Giorgio Cornaro.

1492   *March 25.* Giovanni resumes work on the pictures of the Sala del Maggior Consiglio, together with Alvise Vivarini, Cristoforo Caselli (called "Il Temperelli") from Parma, Lattazio di Rimini, Marco Marziale, Vicenzo della Destre and Francesco Bissolo.

         July 15. Gentile Bellini agrees to execute, together with Giovanni, the large paintings of the Scuola di San Marco.

1496   *November 26.* Alberto da Bologna informs Isabella Gonzaga that Giovanni Bellini has agreed to paint a picture for her famous "studiolo", which is being decorated with the works of Mantegna, Perugino, Costa, Correggio.

1497   *October 4.* When Giovanni refuses to paint a "veduta" of Paris for Francesco Gonzaga — as he had never been there — the painter writes to Gonzaga asking to be allowed to paint a subject of his own choosing.

1499   Death of Aloise Bellini, Giovanni's son.

1502   *December.* Work is under way on the Garzatori altar piece, in the church of Santa Corona in Vicenza.

1501—1506 A significant period for the painter's relations with Isabella Gonzaga. At first, Bellini accepted to paint a picture with a subject indicated beforehand; he goes back on his decision fearing his work would not bear comparison with Mantegna. Isabella, yields, breaking the iconographic pattern for the paintings in her "studiolo", *pur che dipinga qualque historia o fabula, aut de sua inventio ne pinga una che representi cosa antiqua et bello significato* ("that he paints some antique story or fable or one of his own invention with a lofty theme inspired by antiquity"). As the artist does not adhere to these terms either, Isabella falls back on the idea of a *Nativity* in which the figure of John the Baptist should be included. After long hesitations Bellini paints a *Virgin with St. John the Evangelist* and *qualque luntani et altra fantaxia che molto stara'meglio* ("some landscapes and other fantasies which would be much better suited"). In July the picture is completed. The beauty of the picture makes Isabella commission another painting. This time it is Cardinal Bembo who assumes the role of the intermediary. On January 1, 1505, Bembo writes to Isabella: *la invenzione ... bisognera che l'accomodi alla fantaxia di lui ...* ("you will have to leave the choice of the subject to his own fantasy"). The correspondence continues the following year too but the outcome is unknown. It is quite possible that the painting under consideration should be *The Feast of the Gods.*

1505   He dates the *Pala of San Zaccaria* in Venice, *Virgin and Child with Two Saints and a Donor* (Cornbury Park) and St. Jerome (Washington, National Gallery of Art).

1506   *February 7.* Dürer writes from Venice to Pirkheimer about his meeting Giovanni Bellini: *Er ist sehr alt und noch immer der beste in der Malerei* ("He is very old, but he is still the supreme painter"). The same day Giacomo Dolfin mentions in his will that the votive picture in San Francesco della Vigna is being painted.

1507   Recording the death of Gentile in his diary (published only in 1888 in Venice) Marino Sanuto writes: . . . *e restato il fratello Zuan Bellin che è più excellente pittor de Italia* (" . . . there remains his brother Giovanni Bellini, the most brilliant painter of Italy). In the testament dated February 18, Giovanni is entrusted with the task of finishing *St. Mark Preaching at Alexandria* (Brera, Milan).

1507   *September 28.* Giovanni Bellini is entrusted with the task of executing the three pictures for the Sala del Maggior Consiglio left unfinished on account of Aloise Vivarini's death. Carpaccio, Vittore Belliniano and a certain Gerolamo were to work with him. The Portrait of Doge Leonardo Loredan dates from the same year.

1509   *Virgin and Child Blessing* (Detroit, Institute of Arts).

1510   He signs and dates *Virgin and Child Blessing in a Landscape* (Milan, Brera).

1513   Signs and dates the altarpiece in the church of San Giovanni Crisostomo, Venice.

1514   Receives a last payment (85 ducats) from Alfonso d'Este, probably for the *Feast of the Gods*.

1515   February 27. Giovanni continues to work in the Sala del Maggior Consiglio in the Palazzo Ducale.

       July 4. "Messer Zuan Bellin" contracts with the Scuola Grande di San Marco to paint a canvas representing the martyrdom of St. Mark. After the master's death, the work is completed by Vittore Belliniano.

1515   *Nude with Mirror (Toilet of Venus)* (Vienna, Kunsthistorisches Museum) and *Portrait of Fra Teodoro da Urbino* (London, National Gallery).

1516   Signs and dates *Virgin and Child with St. John the Baptist* (Padova, Museo Civico).

1516   November 29. Marino Sanuto notes the following in his diary: *Se intesse, questa matina esser morto Zuan Bellini optimo pytor (. . .) la cui fama è nota per il mondo e cossi vechio come l'era, dipenzeva per excelentia* ("News came this morning of the death of Zuan Bellin excellent painter . . . whose fame spread throughout the world, and though he was very old he painted most excellently.")

ESSENTIAL BIBLIOGRAPHY

R. FRY, *Giovanni Bellini*, London, 1900

G. GRONAU, *Die Künstlerfamilie Bellini*, Leipzig, 1909.

G. B. CAVALCASELLE, J. A. CROWE, *A History of Painting in North Italy* 3 vol., Borenius publishers, London, 1912.

A. VENTURI, *Storia dell'arte italiana*, VII 3—4, Milan, 1914—1915.

L. DUSSLER, *Giovanni Bellini*, Frankfort on the Main, 1935.

R. VAN MERLE, *The Development of the Italian School*, The Hague, 1935.

G. GAMBA, *Giovanni Bellini*, Milan, 1937.

PH. HENDY, L. GOLDSCHEIDER, *Giovanni Bellini*, Oxford-London, 1945.

R. LONGHI, *Viatico per cinque secoli di pittura veneziana*, Florence, 1946.

R. PALLUCCHINI, *Giovanni Bellini*, exhibition catalogue, Venice, 1949.

L. COLETTI, *Pittura veneta del Quattrocento*, Novara, 1953

B. BERENSON, *Italian Pictures of the Renaissance, Venetian School*, London, 1957.

R. PALLUCHINI, *Giovanni Bellini*, Milan, 1959.

G. FIOCCO, *Giovanni Bellini*, Milan, 1960.

F. HEINEMANN, *Bellini e i belliniani*, Venice, 1962

S. BOTTARI, *Giovanni Bellini*, 2 vols., Milan, 1963

M. BONICATTI, *Aspetti dell'Umanesimo nella pittura veneta*, Rome, 1964

C. SEMEZZATO, *Giovanni Bellini*, Florence, 1966

G. ROBERTSON, *Giovanni Bellini*, Oxford, 1968

T. PIGNATTI, *Giovanni Bellini*, Milan, 1969.

LIST OF REPRODUCTIONS

In the text:

PIETÀ
(probably the *Pietà* at Brera)
Pen drawing
13.1 × 18.1 cm.
Paris, The Louvre

PAGAN ALLEGORY
(Attributed to Giovanni Bellini
by numerous researchers)
Distemper on panel
31 × 25 cm.
Florence, Contini-Bonacossi Coll.

*BELLINI'S SIGNATURE ON THE
"FEASTS OF GODS"*
1514
Washington, National Gallery

Plates:

1. TRANSFIGURATION
   1455—1460
   Distemper on panel
   134 × 68 cm.
   Venice, Civico Museo Correr
2. PIETÀ
   1455—1460
   Distemper on panel
   46 × 38 cm.
   Milan, Museo Poldi Pezzoli
3. VIRGIN AND CHILD
   (MADONNA TRIVULZIO)
   1460—1465
   Distemper on panel
   78 × 54 cm.
   Milan, Civiche Raccolte d'Arte
4. PIETÀ
   About 1460
   Distemper on panel
   74 × 50 cm.
   Venice, Civico Museo Correr
   (Dürer's monogram is visible (apochri-
   phal).
5. CRUCIFIXION
   About 1455
   Distemper on panel
   54.5 × 30 cm.
   Venice, Civico Museo Correr

6. AGONY IN THE GARDEN
   About 1459
   Distemper on panel
   81 × 127 cm.
   London, National Gallery
7. THE BLOOD OF THE REDEEMER
   1460—1462
   Distemper on panel
   47 × 34 cm.
   London, National Gallery
8. PIETÀ
   About 1460
   Distemper on panel
   86 × 107 cm.
   Milan, Brera
9. POLYPTYCH OF SAN VINCENZO
   FERRERI
   1464—1468
   Distemper on panel
   Size of the compartments in the upper
   register: 72 × 67 cm.
   Central panel: 167 × 67 cm.
   Compartments of the predella: 36 × 60 cm.
   Venice, Church of SS Giovanni and Paolo
10. PRESENTATION IN THE TEMPLE
    1460—1464
    Distemper on panel
    80 × 105 cm.
    Venice, Querini Stampalia Gallery
11. VIRGIN AND CHILD
    (MADONNA LOCHIS)
    1460—1465
    Distemper on panel
    57 × 34 cm.
    Bergamo, Accademia Carrara
12. PALA DI PESARO
    1471—1475
    Oil on panel
    Pesaro, Musei Civici
    Scene from the predella: *St. Francis in
    Ecstasy*
13. PALA DI PESARO. Predella
    The panel at the base of the pilaster on
    the right: *St. Terentianus*
    43 × 36 cm.
14. PALA DI PESARO. Predella
    The panel at the base of the pilaster on
    the left: *St. George Killing the Dragon*
    43 × 36 cm.

Oil on panel
58 × 107 cm.
Venice, Gallerie dell'Accademia

43. TREE WITH INSCRIPTION,
fragment from a retable
About 1500
Oil on panel
31 × 22 cm.
Venice, Gallerie dell'Accademia

44. PIETÀ
About 1505
Oil on panel
65 × 90 cm.
Venice, Gallerie dell'Accademia

45—46. PALA BARBARIGO
(SACRA CONVERSAZIONE), details
1488
Oil on canvas
200 × 320 cm.
Murano, The Church of San Pietro
Martire

47. SACRA CONVERSAZIONE
(VIRGIN AND CHILD,
SAINT JOHN THE BAPTIST AND A
WOMAN SAINT)
Between 1500—1505
Oil on panel
54 × 76 cm.
Venice, Gallerie dell'Accademia

48. VIRGIN AND CHILD,
SS PETER AND SEBASTIAN
About 1490,
Oil on panel
84 × 61 cm.
Paris, The Louvre

49. RELIGIOUS ALLEGORY
(ALLEGORY OF SOULS IN PURGA-
TORY)
1490—1500
Oil on panel
75 × 119 cm.
Florence, Uffizi

50. THE ASCENSION
1501—1513
Oil on panel
350 × 190 cm.
Murano, The Church of San Pietro
Martire

51. MADONNA OF THE MEADOW
About 1505
Oil on panel transferred to canvas
67 × 89 cm.
London, National Gallery

52. MADONNA OF THE MEADOW,
detail

53. PORTRAIT OF JACOPO
MARCELLO (?)
About 1482—1490
Oil on panel
51 × 37 cm.
Washington, National Gallery of Art
(Kress Donation)

54. FEAST OF THE GODS
1504
Oil on canvas
170 × 188 cm.
Washington, National Gallery of Art

55. NUDE WITH MIRROR
(TOILET OF VENUS) detail
1515
Oil on panel
62 × 79 cm.
Vienna, Kunsthistorisches Museum

56. THE TRIUMPH OF SCIPIO
1507—1508
Oil on canvas
74.8 × 35.6 cm.
Washington, National Gallery of Art
(Kress Donation)

57. THE TRIUMPH OF SCIPIO, detail

58. PORTRAIT OF A YOUTH
About 1500
Oil on panel
34 × 25 cm.
Rome, Capitolina

59. PORTRAIT OF A YOUTH
1500
Oil on panel
32 × 26 cm.
Paris, The Louvre

60. PORTRAIT OF PIETRO BEMBO (?)
detail
1500—1505
Oil on panel
43 × 34 cm.
Hampton Court, British Royal Collec-
tions

61. PALA DI SAN ZACCARIA
(SACRA CONVERSAZIONE)
1505
Oil on panel transferred to canvas
500 × 235 cm.
Venice, Gallerie dell'Accademia
Detail: SS Lucia and Jerome

62. PALA DI SAN ZACCARIA
(SACRA CONVERSAZIONE)
Detail: SS Peter and Catherine

63. PORTRAIT OF DOGE LEONARDO
LOREDAN
About 1501
Oil on panel
61.5 × 45 cm.
London, National Gallery

REPRODUCTIONS

1. Transfiguration
←

2. Pietà
3. Virgin and Child (Madonna Trivulzio)

4. Pietà

8. Pietà

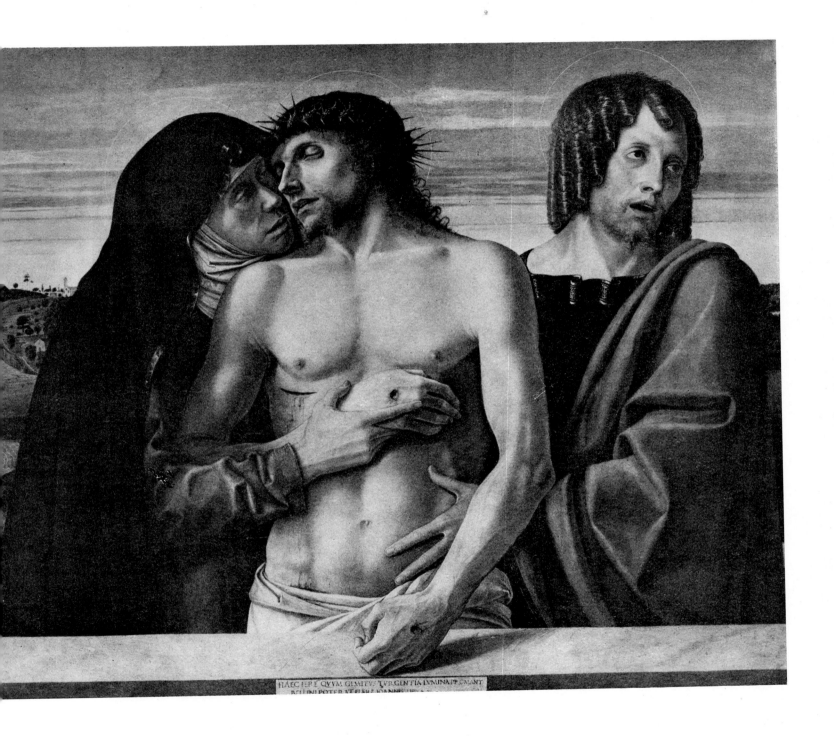

HAEC FERE QVVM GEMITVS TVRGENTIA LVMINA PROMANT
BELLINI POTERAT FLERE IOANNIS OPVS

11. Madonna and Child (Madonna Lochis)

IOANNES BELLINVS

12. Pala di Pesaro *(Scene from the predella:* St. Francis in Ecstasy)

13. Pala di Pesaro *(Scene from the predella:* St. Terentianus)
14. Pala di Pesaro *(Scene from the predella:* St. George Killing the Dragon)

16. Pala di Pesaro *(Cimasa:* Pietà)

17. Madonna and Child (Madonna Greca)

18. Portrait of a Youth
19. Portrait of a Young Senator

22. Virgin and Child (Wyllis Madonna)

23. St. Jerome
24. St. Jerome, *detail*

25—26. St. Francis in Ecstasy, *details*
27. The Annunciation, *detail*

35. Pala di San Giobbe, *detail:* Musical Angel

37. Inconstancy
38. Slander

39. Perseverence
40. Prudence

42. Virgin and Child, SS Catherine and Magdalene

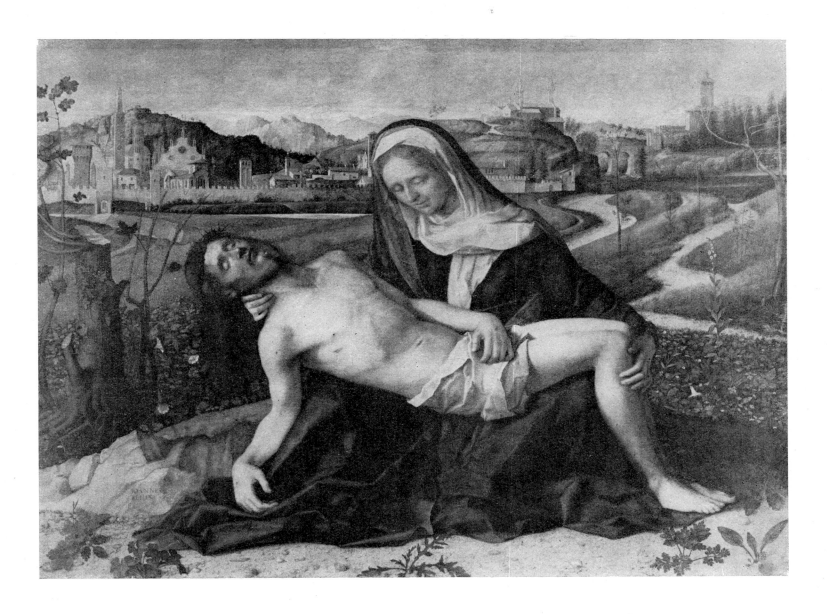

48. Virgin and Child, SS Peter and Sebastian

51. The Madonna of the Meadow

54. Feast of the Gods

55. Nude with Mirror (Toilet of Venus)

56. The Triumph of Scipio
57. The Triumph of Scipio, *detail*

62. Pala di San Zaccaria, *detail:* SS Peter and Catherine

63. Portrait of Doge Leonardo Loredan

MERIDIANE PUBLISHING HOUSE
BUCHAREST
PRINTED IN ROMANIA